101 WACKY SCIENCE JOKES

by Melvin Berger
Illustrated by Rick Mujica

SCHOLASTIC INC.
New York Toronto London Auckland Sydney

ISBN 0-590-42388-6

12   5 6 7 8 9/9

Printed in the U.S.A.   01

First Scholastic printing, November 1989

101
WACKY
SCIENCE
JOKES

LAB LAFFS

A scientist found a way
to make wool out of milk.
There was only one problem —
it made the cow
look sheepish!

Did you hear about the scientist who:
- planted sugar because he wanted to raise cane?
- planted birdseed to grow canaries?
- planted old cars for a bumper crop?

In the middle of an experiment, Professor Zany told his assistant, "I've changed my mind."

"I hope the new one is better than the old one!" answered the assistant.

A biologist was asked the difference between an oak tree and a tight shoe.

"One makes acorns, the other makes corns ache!" she replied.

Professor Zany: I raised a goat without horns.
Scientist: But —
Professor Zany: No butts!

Some boys decided to trick a scientist. They glued together the head of an ant, the wings of a fly, and the legs of a bee.

"What kind of bug is this?" they asked the scientist.

"Did it hum before you caught it?"

"Yes," they answered.

"Then it must be a humbug," the scientist replied.

SILLY SCIENCE SHORTIES

A doctor who treats ducks is a quack!

The planetarium puts on all-star shows!

Local anesthetics are for people who can't afford the imported kind!

The electrician's toast:
More power to you!

The optician's toast:
You haven't seen anything yet!

The electric company turns me on!

The atomic scientist on vacation
has "gone fission"!

14

RIDDLE RIOT

What did one atom say to another atom?

Nothing. Atoms can't talk!

Feed it and it lives. Give it water and it dies. What is it?

Fire!

Why does the giraffe have such a long neck?

Because his head is so far from his body!

What is the difference between the North Pole and the South Pole?

The whole world!

Which travels faster, heat or cold?

Heat, because you can easily catch cold!

What do you call two germs living together?

Cellmates!

Where does the witch keep her spaceship?

In the broom closet!

When does it rain money?

When there's some change in the weather!

What are five things that contain milk?

Butter, cheese, ice cream — and two cows!

What are the world's three zones?

Arctic, Temperate, and Tow Away!

What did one magnet say to
another?

I find you very attractive!

What do zebras have that no other animals have?

Little zebras!

What steps would you take if you suddenly smelled poison gas?

Very big ones!

COMPUTER QUICKIES

What did the computer say to the scientist?

You can count on me!

Computer technician: I know a computer that can think faster than three men.

Young woman: I'd rather have the three men!

One day the scientist came home very tired. His wife asked, "Did you have a hard day at the lab, dear?"

"I sure did," he answered. "The computer broke down — and I had to think!"

Soon after takeoff, a voice came over the plane's public-address system. "Ladies and gentlemen, this is a special plane. There is no pilot on board. The plane is being run by a computer. There is absolutely nothing to worry about . . . nothing to worry about . . . nothing to worry about. . . ."

DAFFY-NITIONS

Parasite: A person who lives in Paris.

Copper ore: Something used to paddle a copper boat.

Continental shelf: A place where the oceans keep their extra water.

Octopus: An eight-sided cat.

Astronaut: Someone who is glad to be down and out.

Archaeologist: A scientist whose career is in ruins; a rubble rouser.

Astronomer: A night watchman.

Pollution: Grime in the streets.

Centigrade: Mailed out a report card.

Fahrenheit: Not too short, not too tall.

Launch: An astronaut's favorite meal.

Dry dock: A thirsty physician.

Geologist: A fault finder.

Ice: Skid stuff.

Rhubarb: Celery with high blood pressure.

Satellite: Something to put on a horse if you're riding at night.

Flood: A river that's too big for its bridges.

Volcano: A mountain that blew its stack.

X ray: Another name for bellyvision.

MERRY MIX-UPS

What do you get when you cross . . .

. . . a computer and a rubber band?

I don't know what it's called. But it makes snap decisions!

. . a flea and a rabbit?

Bugs Bunny!

. . . a pine tree and an apple tree?

A tree that grows pineapples!

. . . an elephant and a Boy Scout?

An elephant that helps old ladies cross the street.

. . . a termite and a praying mantis?

A bug that says grace before eating your house!

. . . a parrot and a gorilla?

A bird that says, "Polly wants a cracker — NOW!"

. . . an elephant and a jar of peanut butter?

Either peanut butter with a wonderful memory, or an elephant that sticks to the roof of your mouth!

. . . a stereo and a refrigerator?

A concert of cool music!

... a clock and a chicken?

An alarm cluck!

... a duck and a cow?

Quackers and milk!

MORE RIDDLE RIOT

Why was Newton surprised when
he was hit on the head by an apple?

He was sitting under a pear tree!

What is long, yellow, and always points north?

A magnetic banana!

What did the mountain say to the earthquake?

It's not my fault!

What happens if you throw a yellow rock into the Red Sea?

It gets wet!

Why is touching an electric wire like using a credit card?

They both give you a charge!

How can you make a fire with only one stick?

Make sure the stick is a match!

Why does the stork raise one leg?

If it raised both legs, it would fall!

Why are fish good at science?

They spend all of their time in schools!

If we breathe oxygen in the daytime, what do we breathe at night?

Nitrogen!

What kind of jokes do scientists tell?

Wisecracks!

MEDICAL MADNESS

Patient: It hurts every time I raise my arm. What should I do?

Doctor: Don't raise your arm.

Patient: My memory is terrible. I forget everything. I lost my job. I have no friends. Can you help me?

Doctor: How long have you had this problem?

Patient: What problem?

Doctor: Your cough sounds better today.
Patient: It should. I practiced it all night.

Patient: Nobody ever listens to me.
Psychiatrist: Thank you. Next patient.

Patient: I feel dizzy for an hour after I get up in the morning. What should I do?
Doctor: Get up an hour later.

Doctor to elderly patient: You're going to live until you're 80.
Elderly patient: But I am 80.
Doctor: There, I told you so!

Patient: What causes baldness?
Doctor: Lack of hair.

The eye doctor's theme song:
"Oh, Say Can You See?"

When is the vet the busiest?

When it rains cats and dogs.

Psychiatrist: What's your problem?
Kangaroo: I feel jumpy.

Psychiatrist: What's your problem?

Porcupine: I'm on pins and needles.

Why is a surgeon like a comedian?

They both leave people in stitches.

Why do surgeons wear masks?

If they make a mistake, no one will know who did it.

Why did a doctor keep her
bandages in the refrigerator?

To use them for cold cuts.

Father: My son thinks he's a hen.
Psychiatrist: How long has this
  been going on?
Father: About two years.
Psychiatrist: Why didn't you come
  to me sooner?
Father: We needed the eggs.

Doctor: Are you taking the cough medicine I gave you?

Patient: No. After tasting it, I decided I'd rather cough!

Did you hear about the patient who acted silly in the eye doctor's office?

He made a spectacle of himself!

RIB TICKLERS

Why is winter the best time to buy thermometers?

Because they're a lot higher in the summer.

Student: Which is more important to us, the sun or the moon?

Professor Zany: The moon.

Student: Why?

Professor Zany: The moon gives us light at night when we need it. The sun only gives light in the daytime when we don't need it.

What's the best way to prevent
infection caused by biting insects?

Don't bite any.

Why did the chicken cross the road?

For fowl purposes.

Scientist: I heard a funny joke at the lab.
Scientist's wife: Tell it to me.
Scientist: No, that's carrying a joke too far!

Judy: That's a dogwood tree.
Jan: How do you know?
Judy: By its bark.

Business is . . .

. . . "looking up," said the
astronomer.

. . . "looking better," said the
optician.

. . . "growing," said the biologist.

Why are people shocked by lightning?

Because it doesn't know how to conduct itself.

How do you know Professor Zany is a real blockhead?

Because he gets a splinter whenever he scratches his head!

Professor Zany hooked up all of the appliances in his house to one electronic control panel. By mistake he crossed the wires for his electric blanket and his toaster. Now whenever he goes to sleep at night, he keeps popping out of bed!

Scientist's daughter: I saw a baby snake today.

Scientist: How did you know it was a baby?

Scientist's daughter: It had a rattle!

The boy asked his father, "What is electricity?"

"I don't know," his father said.

A few minutes later the boy asked, "What makes it rain?"

"I don't know," his father replied.

Once more the boy began, "What causes — " but he stopped.

"Ask your question," his father urged. "How else are you going to learn?"

CLASSROOM COMEDY

Teacher: What is true of all the
scientists of the 17th century?
Student: They're all dead.

Teacher: A grasshopper can jump four feet in the air.

Student: So what? A wasp can make a grown man jump eight feet!

Teacher: Use *camphor* in a sentence.

Student: Last year I went to camp for the summer.

Teacher: Oxygen was discovered in 1773.

Student: What did people breathe before then?

Teacher: What are the four seasons?

Student: Salt, pepper, mustard, and ketchup!

Teacher: You should become an oceanographer.

Student: Why?

Teacher: Because all your marks are below C level.

Student: Would you be angry with me for something I didn't do?

Teacher: Of course not.

Student: Well, I didn't do my science homework!

Teacher: How many lengths of string does it take to reach the moon?

Student: Only one *very* long one!

Teacher: How can you make antifreeze?
Student: Steal her blanket!

Teacher: What liquid will never freeze?
Student: Hot water!

Teacher: Why do birds fly south every winter?
Student: It's too far to walk.

SPACE SILLIES

Stan: Why did the astronomer hit himself on the head with a hammer one afternoon?

Sam: So he could see stars during the day.

After eating his first meal on the moon, the astronaut reported, "The food was good, but the place lacked atmosphere."

Why is an astronaut like a football player?

They both want touchdowns!

Student: How can we know if a message we send into space is being received?

Professor Zany: That's easy. Send it collect and see if they pay.

Professor Zany: What was the name of the first satellite to orbit the earth?
Student: The moon!

Student: What keeps the moon in place?
Professor Zany: Its beams.

Mrs. Jones: My daughter's going to become an astronaut.

Mrs. Smith: How do you know?

Mrs. Jones: Her teacher says she just takes up space.

Which are the most dangerous stars?

Shooting stars!

Sam: Did you hear the joke about the sun?

Stan: No.

Sam: I'd better not tell it to you. It's over your head.